BECOMING A
WORSHIP PASTOR

CALEB HOLGERSON

To Kate. You challenged, encouraged, and supported me the entire way. I couldn't have done this without you. Thank you for always believing in me.

CONTENTS

Introduction

A little while back I had a shift in thinking regarding the way I viewed my role as a worship leader. Leading songs had kind of lost its appeal and although I still loved music, I knew there was something greater I was missing. I didn't go into ministry to sing songs. I never led worship because it was my only outlet for music. Music wasn't what it was about for me; but unfortunately, that's what it had come down to. I started in ministry because I wanted to see lives changed. I wanted to see Jesus work in communities. I wanted to help people. I wanted to be a pastor. But I was just a musician. I fear that is a common struggle.

I'm a young guy, a young pastor. I don't have a long drawn out saga of a story about building a huge ministry, getting burned out, and starting over at the basics. I'm regular guy, who started leading worship in high school because I connected with Jesus in worship. The shift happened when I realized what changed in my life through worship wasn't changing in other's lives when I led worship.

The reason lives weren't changing is because I was just singing songs and assuming worship was happening. I was a leader of songs instead being a leader of people. I wasn't cultivating an atmosphere of worship. I wasn't pastoring in worship. I was singing songs and hoping the lyrics and pad sounds from the keyboard would do that.

When I had this shift in thinking, I realized that songs don't pastor people. That's my job. Leading worship is a pastoral role. I needed to become a better pastor. From that point, I began to evaluate every aspect of my job, from auditions to rehearsals to Sunday morning, and consider how I could pastor in those areas. I began to consider how I could lead and develop people well by finding their gifts and helping them to use those gifts for the glory of God.

That's what this book is about. It's an evaluation of the worship leader's role and an implementation of how to pastor in that role. My hope is that what you find in the pages to come will help to change your mindset, as it did for me, regarding your role as a worship leader. My hope is that worship leaders would become worship pastors.

This is not a book about stripping away the lights, synths, or ambient sounds of a service. It's a book about how to use those things as tools for the gospel, tools for the spiritual growth of the Church. It's a book about leading the church in psalms, hymns, and spiritual songs by speaking to the church in songs, hymns, and spiritual songs, as the Apostle Paul instructs in Ephesians 5:19. It's about knowing the people and the prayers of your church and learning how to lead those people and speak into those prayers.

Initially, when I started writing, I was just trying to organize my thoughts for worship leaders that I am developing; However, the more I wrote, the more I realized there are other worship leaders out there that need to learn how to pastor. Hopefully many who want to learn how to pastor.

I believe the Church needs more worship pastors. The Church needs more pastors who are able to communicate worship. For thousands of years, followers of God have worshipped through song, yet many believers still do not understand it. All too often worship services are seen as an opener for a sermon. Although I never want to downplay the preaching of the gospel, I believe the Church is missing something when it opts out of worship. The Church is missing something when worship is seen as a concert before the important part.

I've found that passionate worship takes place where people are pastored in worship. When pastored in

3

worship, churches begin to understand its importance. When pastored in worship, followers of Jesus begin to recognize the presence of God. When pastored in worship, lives begin to change. As I've begun to pastor in worship, I have seen just that.

Romans 12: 6-8 says this:

" [6] We have different gifts, according to the grace given to each of us. If your gift is prophesying, then prophesy in accordance with your faith; [7] if it is serving, then serve; if it is teaching, then teach; [8] if it is to encourage, then give encouragement; if it is giving, then give generously; if it is to lead, do it diligently; if it is to show mercy, do it cheerfully."

In my very loose translation of this verse it is saying, whatever you do, do it well. If it is to lead, do it diligently. Do it with care and persistence. Paul is telling us to put thought into our leadership, to put thought into our ministry.

My challenge to the worship leader reading this book is to change your mindset. Force a shift in thinking. Lead with diligence. Become a pastor of people instead of a leader of songs.

VISION
Chapter One

When I was 18 years old I picked up a worship leading gig at a small rural church plant. I actually found the opening on craigslist. The post was short, stating that a small church was looking for musicians and someone to lead them. I, having led worship teams all through high school and at the time being in bible college, thought this would be a great opportunity to boost my resume and gain experience. So I emailed the pastor, met him for lunch, and led worship at the church the following Sunday.

I walked in on my first Sunday, met the volunteer team and got set up for service. It was a small service, but a good message and kind people. But something seemed to be missing. I had a funny feeling. Something was off. And it wasn't just weird people that you sometimes meet in churches. This church was lacking something.

I stayed there for about 3 months. I showed up, led worship, talked with people and went home. I began to notice sermons were often unprepared, outreach events were put in place more or less to be social gatherings, and congregants weren't really going anywhere spiritually. That realization pointed to the problem. There was no vision. There was no real goal for the church. Church was just something that we were doing, an event we were putting on.

Although it didn't turn out to be a great resume builder, I did gain experience. And I learned a valuable lesson: Vision is imperative to ministry. Without vision there is no direction. Without vision there is no goal. Vision is the why behind the what. Without a why your what is meaningless.

Proverbs 29:18 says, "without vision people perish, but he who keeps the law will be blessed."

I love the way the Message Bible puts it: "If people can't see what God is doing, they stumble all over themselves; But when they attend to what He reveals, they are most blessed."

After studying this verse, I began to ask myself how I was attending to what God had revealed to me in and about worship. How was I, a pastor, a shepherd of people, sharing vision for the area I pastor in? How could I avoid being what I was bothered by when working for the church plant? I began to study vision and consider the purpose of my leadership and the teams I lead.

Vision, as we'll define it here, is the ideal image of what the future could be like. Vision is the direction in which you are leading. For the worship pastor, vision is the ideal image of your team and how it operates, ministers together, and plays together musically. It's also the ideal image of your church, how it worships, and how it relates **to God.**

The ideal image of the future of worship in my current church is to be a worshiping church, passionate about the presence of God. That is the vision. That is the direction in which I am leading. That is the ultimate goal.

To effectively lead in that direction, I need help. My worship team needs to be on board. Vision always starts with those closest to me. Vision starts with the team. My worship team is made up of parents, students, small group leaders and spouses of other pastors. There is a wide range of ages, ethnicities and life stages represented on my team. The same wide range that is represented in my church. My team touches nearly every demographic in my church. Realizing this made it clear to me that teams are carriers of vision. This means that growing my team spiritually will grow my church spiritually.

When my team takes hold of vision, it spreads to my entire church. I'm casting vision to students who are taking that vision with them to youth groups. I'm casting vision to small group leaders who are taking it with them to their group. I'm casting vision to parents who are taking it to their kids. I'm casting vision to husbands and wives who take it to their spouses. From there, vision continues to spread. That's huge, but in order to do that I first have to reach my team.

Growing your team starts with knowing your team. You've probably heard the old adage, "people don't care how much you know until they know how much you care." There's some truth to that. People will pay attention to your leadership, to your vision, when they know they matter to you. I learned this early on through a conversation with a mentor, Kurtis.

Building Influence

Kurtis and I sat down outside of a coffee shop in Washington, D.C. and I told him all about the worship pastor position I was about to step into. We discussed the vision of the church, the heart of the lead pastor, and the worship team I would be leading. After several minutes of hearing the exciting stuff, he asked, "What are you not excited about? What struggles do you foresee?" I wasn't exactly ready for that question. I really just wanted to talk about the fun stuff. Looking back, I'm glad he asked.

I told him I wasn't excited about building influence in a new team and a new church. I explained that I had been part of teams before where a new leader came in and they never ended up clicking. They were a bad fit. They weren't influential, they weren't visionary, and they didn't move people. I didn't want to end up like that, but I didn't know where to start.

I knew there was a need to build influence, and I thought it was best if I could do that relatively quickly. I recognized that casting vision without first building influence was meaningless. Influence is the ability to effect the character, development or behavior of something or someone. As a pastor, I'm in the people development business. In order to develop someone spiritually, not to mention an entire congregation, I need to be able to connect with them and influence them. I need to be able to cast vision they can grab onto.

Kurtis' response, I believe, made all the difference in my first few months at the new church. "Buy them pizza" is what he told me. "Within your first month gather everyone on your team, buy them pizza, and just hang out with them." So I did.

A few weeks after starting in my new position, I gathered everyone on my worship team together for a meal. It took forever for the pizza to get there. It was Sunday afternoon, we had just led worship for 3 services, and everyone was tired and hungry. It wasn't the start I was looking for. Luckily though, most of the team had known each other for several years, so people were hanging out and having a good time. Praise God. Because I had no idea what to talk to these people about.

When the pizza finally came, everyone gathered together, began to eat and continued to talk. I, for the most part, just listened. There, I learned another valuable lesson: Know your team and you'll know your church.

By just letting everyone talk, I learned what they value. I learned what they love about the church. I learned their hearts for the people around them. And I learned their dreams for the worship department. By listening to the hearts of my team, I was listening to an already existing vision. Some of them spoke of life change, some of seeing the Spirit of God move in services, and others about writing songs and building up musicians. There was a clear desire to lead well and to be led well. There was an obvious passion for worship. And there was a God given dream in each of them for where we could go. When the team began to open up about these things, I was able to speak into it, dream with them, and in doing so, begin to build, influence, and capture a vision for the future.

Our vision, to build a worshiping church, passionate about the presence of God, came out of two places. First, the conversations with my worship team over pizza. Second, the church's overall vision.

Through conversation with the team, I learned what the church is passionate about and what the church is worshiping God for. That's an important thing to know as their worship pastor. My church loves to see evidence of the power of God. They love to see the Holy Spirit move in a service and in their lives. That's where the second part of our vision statement comes from. The "passionate about the presence of God" part. Some of our church is already there. I want to take the whole church there. And I want to go deeper with the individuals that are already passionate about God's presence.

The first part of our vision statement, "building a worshiping church," comes from our church's overall vision: "We want everyone to find a life worth living by learning to invest everything in a relationship with Jesus." We believe that worship is an essential piece of a relationship with Jesus. In the Greek, the word worship comes from two words meaning "toward" and "kiss." To worship is to "kiss toward" God. An intimate act. An act signifying a deep relationship.

Combining the two pieces of our vision statement, you could say that our vision is to put people in relationship with God and for them to love being in that relationship. Going back to Proverbs 29:18, "If people can't see what God is doing, they stumble all over themselves; But when they attend to what He reveals, they are most blessed," the vision that has been revealed is to build a worshiping church. The hard work comes in attending to it. Honestly, I struggle with this part the most, but I go off of the example of a previous church I worked at. They funnel vision through 3 lengths of time: yearly, monthly and weekly.

Breaking Down the Vision

Start by looking at your vision and what piece of it you can achieve over the next year. At this church, we used one word or a simple phrase to sum it up. This yearly vision piece is fairly big and broad.

For instance, one year we decided it was important that our team find greater value in servanthood. We decided that by the end of the next year, we wanted to see a clear change in how our team served the church, the community, and each other. Our ultimate goal here was to build great leaders. We recognized the fact that great leaders are great servants.

Our phrase for the year was "only servants." The idea was that we are servants first and specialists second. We have gifts and talents that we specialize in, but as followers of Christ, we are to use them to serve other people. Through monthly strategy, we saw movement in our yearly vision.

Our monthly strategy kept us focused. One night

every month our team would gather together for a meal, fellowship, and a short teaching. These occasions were incredible opportunities for vision casting. During the teaching portion of the evening, our speakers would concentrate on great acts of service in the bible and how service is ministry's truest form, how those who serve connect with Jesus in a very real way.

In this time, we also gave opportunities to partner with other ministries. We talked about missions and upcoming trips, we discussed involvement in local ministries that our church had relationships with, and we brainstormed ways to support the other ministries of our church. Several times throughout the year, we asked the entire team to serve together in an outside ministry. This monthly focus had a massive impact on weekly services.

I stated above that those who serve connect with Jesus in a very real way. We saw that to be true in our weekly services. In making a lifestyle of servanthood, our team saw weekend services in a new light. They began to see new opportunities to connect with the congregation. They began to see where they could minister to individual people. They even began to play better musically because they saw the importance of music as a tool for ministry. They began to see everything we did together as an opportunity to serve.

If there is anything I want you to take away from

reading this, it's this: Have a clear vision and learn how to attend to it. I believe that doing so is essential to   pastoring well. It shows you where you're going and gives you a reason to do what you're doing.

Proverbs 21:5 says, "good planning and hard work lead to prosperity, but hasty shortcuts lead to poverty." Pastors have spiritual leadership over their congregations. Steward spiritual leadership well by planning well. Laying out vision for your church lays out a plan, which leads to success. It's impossible to measure success if you don't know what you are aiming for. Success here means spiritual growth and an understanding of worship. Starting with the goal, the vision, allows you to lay out a plan.

In the coming chapters, we'll discuss practical ways to pastor your congregation and fulfill your vision for worship.

What to Remember

Vision gives life. (see proverbs 29:18)

Vision is the direction in which you are leading.

Vision gives you a goal. A goal gives you a plan.

Teams are carriers of vision.

Know your team and you'll know your church.

Timothy and Barnabas
Chapter Two

Nathan is one of the greatest mentors I have ever had. He was the worship leader at a church I attended as well as the communications director for another ministry. Recently, he stepped out of his role as the communications director and into a new role in the organization. When I asked him how the new role was going, he said it was great, that in anything he was doing, his job stayed the same. Nathan's exact words were, "I'm here to make disciples."

What I love about Nathan is that that statement really does sum up everything he does. He's constantly bringing people along, pouring into them and sending them off. Nathan is the greatest example of a disciple maker I know. That's what makes him a great leader and a great pastor. It's not his skill or even his knowledge of the bible. Although skill and knowledge are necessary, those traits are not what makes Nathan stand out. It's his desire to grow people. He's in the people development business.

Being a disciple of Jesus means being a student of Jesus. One who studies Him. Each of Jesus' 12 disciples spent 3 years studying Him. They watched Him, ate with Him, listened to Him and as a result became like Him. In fact, that was the entire goal of spending time with Him. When a first century Jewish man wanted to follow a rabbi, he was expected to live with the rabbi 24 hours a day, learning from his every move. A disciple's calling was to walk in the dust of the rabbi, meaning that he was to walk so closely behind the rabbi that he would be covered in the dirt his rabbi kicked up. The hope was that by following so closely and watching his every move, the disciple would become like the rabbi. That's exactly what Christ's disciples did. They walked in His dust.

As pastors, we should be doing the same: bringing people along with us and showing them the way. That's called discipleship. Discipleship is defined as teaching one person the doctrines of another. In the case of the Christian, it is one person teaching another the ways of Jesus. Discipleship isn't just key to ministry, it is ministry. It's growing people and when done properly, it's growing people who grow people. It's creating leaders who create leaders.

Jesus brought His disciples along and then He sent them out. Then Jesus left, He was crucified, resurrected, and ascended. You know the story. But that didn't stop the ministry. In fact, it was just the beginning because Jesus grew leaders who grew leaders. Jesus was a disciple maker who made disciple makers.

Just as it does with vision, discipleship starts with the team. In fact, the team should the main focus of discipleship for the worship pastor. Looking to Jesus as the example, we see that He had lots of followers, but He put His focus on a few. There may be a lot of people in a church, but a disciple maker will focus on discipling a few. For the worship pastor, it's your team. Worship pastors spend more time with the worship team than they do with any other group of people in the church. So the worship pastor's focus should be on taking every opportunity possible to pour into the team. We should be leaders who create leaders.

Rehearsals

Everyone who walks through the front doors on Sunday morning sees the worship team. For that reason, I want my team to lead well. In order to do that, they need to be led well. They need to be discipled. They need to know their role in the church. The number one way I disciple my team is through our weekly rehearsal time.

Rehearsals are an integral part of leading an effective

worship ministry. For me, they have become key factor not only in how I lead worship, but in how I pastor people, cast vision, and build effective teams. I began to value rehearsals when I realized that rehearsals were opportunities for both practical and spiritual development. Rehearsals are weekly opportunities for discipleship.

I used to hate rehearsals. Don't get me wrong, I wanted the team to sound good, we all want that. But I didn't think showing up on Thursday night after a long day of work and playing through the same old songs over and over was worth it. I thought, "let's just get it close and we'll figure out the rest on Sunday morning." But then, after a short spree of not-so-worshipful worship services, I learned to value them.

Practically, rehearsals are an opportunity to get the music right before Sunday morning. That's huge. Practice, however, is what you do on your own. My team lives by the mantra "practice is what happens before rehearsal." Practice is where you prepare your part. And where you prepare your heart. Rehearsal is where we put all the parts together. It's where we ensure that keys and guitar parts don't clash, that background vocalists are singing the best possible harmonies and that dynamics are right and breaks and transitions are tight.

What we have realized is that if everyone is learning their parts at rehearsal, we have to push all the other stuff back to Sunday morning. If we don't have enough time to nail down everything on Sunday morning, our services suffer. If our services suffer, we are not leading well. We cease to be an effective team. When we come into rehearsals prepared; however, I can take my focus off of music and put it on discipleship. When we come into rehearsals prepared, we lead well on Sunday morning. When I don't have to focus on the music, I can place my focus on the team.

Rehearsals are a weekly opportunity for me to connect with my team outside of the hustle of Sunday morning. They allow me to be a part of the lives of those on my team. They are a prime opportunity for us to fellowship, pray, and of course, worship. Being that our rehearsals are toward the end of the week, I often hear of the struggles and celebrations of the week. I know where people are coming from when preparing to lead. Knowing these things makes me a better pastor. It shows me how I can lead my team better.

At the end of every rehearsal, I gather my worship team together for 10 to 15 minutes to share with them a specific vision for the weekend and what to be praying for. It's a moment every week to align our hearts and refocus our purpose. We believe that what we want to see happen in our church, our community and the world begins with us. When I do this, I'm sharing with my team their role in our ministry. I'm taking a moment to focus on discipleship.

To grow my team's leadership capacity in rehearsals, I routinely ask team members to lead devotionals and to pray over the church and team as a whole. I have given new vocalists opportunities to try leading songs and I have started musicians in music directing roles. I've found that there is an abundance of discipleship opportunity associated with rehearsals. When I steward these opportunities well, leaders grow quickly.

Find a Timothy

As leaders begin to grow, I am always searching for one or two people to pour into a little more, to develop a little further. I'm looking for people who have a greater desire for growth and a heart for worship. Often this is someone who is maybe just a step or two behind me in skill or training, but often someone who is way beyond me in potential. This is kind of "Paul and Timothy" idea. I'm searching for those who I can spend time developing further.

When I first started in pastoral ministry, a very wise pastor told me this, "At some point in your ministry, you will find there is someone under your leadership who has more anointing than you do. Learn to lead them well." To be honest, at first, that thought scared me. Partly, because I probably wanted to be the most anointed pastor on the planet, but more so because I knew I wasn't. And I wasn't sure I had the capacity or the character to lead someone with a greater anointing. After the initial fright wore off though, I began to see this as a challenge. I began looking for people with more anointing than I have. People with more skill, talent, and potential than I have.

Currently, I have a worship leader serving under me who is more skilled, more talented and, I believe, more anointed than I am. He has all the pieces he needs in order to lead worship well, pastor well, and see people come to Jesus. He just needs help putting the pieces together. That's my job in discipling him – to give him practical tools to lead the church.

Stephen is an incredible guitar player, a gifted music director, and a passionate worship leader. He genuinely loves Jesus, the Church, and seeing people find life in Christ. The only things he needs help with are casting vision to the team and speaking that vision over the church. The way I develop him is by walking him through how I do it. We frequently have conversations about the vision for a weekend and how to share that vision with the team. I show him how vision flows through everything from building a set to rehearsals to Sunday morning. And then I give him opportunities to build the set that way and cast vision to the team. As far as speaking it over the church goes, I often give Stephen opportunities to pray or speak between songs. Stephen is constantly growing because I am constantly giving him opportunities to grow. I am giving him the tools he needs to lead well.

Soon, Stephen will be transitioning into a campus worship leader role for a new campus our church is planting. Over the last few months as we've been preparing for this transition, Stephen and I have discussed many aspects of worship leading, including becoming a disciple maker. Basically, everything that I've been showing him, he's to show someone else. We've even brainstormed who that person could be as we have built his new team. He's a leader who will soon be creating leaders. A growing person who will soon be growing people.

This is important because growing leaders grow the team both spiritually and practically. Growing the team grows the church. Growing the church is our ultimate goal. Discipleship is how Jesus started the Church. It's why His disciples wrote the gospels. It's how Christianity has always spread.

The apostle Paul is one of the greatest disciple makers of all time. He traveled the world evangelizing, planting churches, and growing and instructing believers. The churches that he was instructing could be considered teams. The teaching was both important for growth and broad enough to touch everyone in the church. Paul could not take the time to pour into everyone on the team one on one; However, he did narrow his discipleship down to one person to spend time developing: Timothy.

Timothy was Paul's right hand. He traveled with him, planted churches with him, and taught with him. Timothy was a student of Paul's work. He was learning to build the Church. As a result of his eagerness to learn, Paul sent Timothy to the Corinth and Philippi on his behalf to teach and correct the believers. Doing so built Timothy's influence in the Church, it connected him to other ministry leaders and it gave him new opportunities to serve and work in his giftings. Those are the goals of discipleship. Discipleship is teaching one person the doctrines of Jesus so that they can influence the church, grow leaders, and find and serve in their giftings.

Find a Barnabas

When I was working with Nathan, he was constantly connecting me to people and to opportunities in order to clarify and develop my gifts. At the time that Nathan came into my life, I had all but failed out of college, I was working a dead end job, and I was far from the goal I had of becoming a pastor. I was frustrated with where I was at, but I didn't know how to move forward. Over the course of several meetings I had expressed these things to Nathan and one day at lunch, everything changed. He suggested a way to finish school that I hadn't thought of. Then he even started making phone calls to get me started before I had the opportunity to change my mind. After that, he connected me to an opportunity with a ministry. Within nine months of that conversation, I was finishing school and stepping into my first role in full time ministry.

Nathan was a Barnabas to me. Barnabas was the apostle Paul's mentor. After his conversion, Barnabas took Paul under his wing. Initially, the disciples were afraid of Paul. Because of his past, as Saul, many feared he was not actually a believer and was attempting to fool them. But Barnabas walked with Paul. He protected him from the Jews, taught with him and encouraged him. In fact, the name Barnabas means Son of Encouragement. I don't believe that Barnabas' name's meaning is a coincidence. I believe it is a biblical directive to disciple makers to be encouraging.

That said, disciple makers also need encouragement. All ministers of the gospel should have both a Barnabas and a Timothy. Someone to guide them and help them as well someone that they are guiding and helping. Someone who is a few steps ahead of them and someone who is a few steps behind. This ensures that pastors have pastors, that disciples are continually growing and are always being poured into. Proverbs 12:15 says, "the way of a fool is right in his own eyes, but a wise man is he who listens to counsel." Always have a counselor. Always be seeking leaders to learn from. Always be seeking leaders to teach.

Discipleship is the most effective tool there is for Kingdom growth. Discipleship is how early leaders operated, how the early church operated, and how we should operate now. Discipleship brings students along, builds them up, and sends them out. Discipleship spreads the gospel of Jesus. Through discipleship is how we should be pastoring.

What to Remember

As pastors, we are in the people development business. Our job is to make disciples.

Discipleship isn't just key to ministry, it is ministry.

Become a disciple maker who makes disciple makers.

Take every possible opportunity to pour into your team.

Find a Timothy. Have someone you can pour into.

Find a Barnabas. Have someone who can pour into you.

Discipleship is how Christianity has always spread.

Lead as Levites
Chapter Three

As a worship pastor, the most effective way to minister to a congregation is by developing a team of ministers, a team of leaders who have the same goals but different strengths. As we've talked about before, vision starts with the team so you need to disciple your team well. The best way that I know to develop a team or a person is by finding a biblical model. For worship teams, our biblical model is found in 1 Chronicles with a Tribe of Israel, known as the Levites.

The Tribe of Levi was the tribe appointed for care of the temple. The Levites were dispersed among the other tribes in order to carry out the functions of the temple in different territories. Their jobs were many as we see in 1 Chronicles 9:26-33:

" [26] But the four principal gatekeepers, who were Levites, were entrusted with the responsibility for the rooms and treasuries in the house of God. [27] They would spend the night stationed around the house of God, because they had to guard it; and they had charge of the key for opening it each morning. [28] Some of them were in charge of the articles used in the temple service; they counted them when they were brought in and when they were taken out. [29] Others were assigned to take care of the furnishings and all the other articles of the sanctuary, as well as the special flour and wine, and the olive oil, incense and spices. [30] But some of the priests took care of mixing the spices. [31] A Levite named Mattithiah, the firstborn son of Shallum the Korahite, was entrusted with the responsibility for baking the offering bread. [32] Some of the Kohathites, their fellow Levites, were in charge of preparing for every Sabbath the bread set out on the table. [33] Those who were musicians, heads of Levite families, stayed in the rooms of the temple and were exempt from other duties because they were responsible for the work day and night."

As caregivers of the temple, the Levites ensured that there was always an atmosphere of worship. Day and night they were responsible for the work. Obviously, because we are studying pastoring in worship and developing a worship team, I want to focus in on the last portion of this passage, about musicians, but I don't want to overlook the other responsibilities of the Levites.

As we are developing our teams to be as the Levites were, the other responsibilities take on more importance. They cared for every aspect of temple worship. As "modern day Levites" the job hasn't changed, the temple has. The Levites were charged with care of the temple, the building. We are charged with care of the Temple of the Holy Spirit, the people. When we're developing our teams as Levites, we are leading them in caring for the Church, the people of God.

The Levites knew the temple inside and out so they knew the work that needed to be done, from guarding and unlocking it to mixing spices and baking bread. In a similar fashion, we should know our people in order to know the work that needs to be done. This is where we move from pastoring a team to pastoring a church. By developing a team as Levites we are developing a team of ministers that connects with the Church, loves them, and genuinely worships when leading them.

Connecting with the Church

It is with purpose that I put "connecting with the church" first on that list. Everything else flows out of that connection. Influence is built through relationship. Your worship team should spend time connecting with the congregation. First and foremost, I encourage my team to attend services. All too often, a worship team is seen on stage and then not seen again until the end of service. I think that is a mistake. The worship team, the leaders of worship, should be leaders in all aspects of a service. Worship leaders should be leaders in note taking. Worship leaders should be leaders in giving. Worship leaders should be leaders in prayer. They should be engaged in every aspect of the service. You cannot lead a church if you do not know what is happening in the church.

My friend Sean is one of the best when it comes to being engaged in a service. Sean was a drummer on my team and at different points was the only drummer on the team. He played in three services every weekend and often for events. Regardless of whether or not he was playing or how many weeks in a row he had played, Sean was in service and was very clearly engaged. He could be seen actively worshiping, nodding along with the sermon, and talking with people after service. Sean also led a small group. He had several families that he would meet with, pray with and walk with on a regular basis. These things are what make him an effective worship leader. It isn't his skill level as a drummer, although that is important and in his case is very high, that makes him a minister. His engagement, his love for our congregation, is.

Love the Church

Just as important as engaging the congregation in a service is engaging with individuals after a service. This is where love comes in. The greatest measure of how well you are loving someone is how well you are praying for them. A worship team should be actively seeking out the needs of the congregation. If you know where there's a need, you'll know where to lead.

Engaging individuals should lead to prayer and praise. The Apostle Paul demonstrates this in Ephesians 1:15-18:

"[15] For this reason, ever since I heard about your faith in the Lord Jesus and your love for all God's people, [16] I have not stopped giving thanks for you, remembering you in my prayers. [17] I keep asking that the God of our Lord Jesus Christ, the glorious Father, may give you the Spirit of wisdom and revelation, so that you may know him better. [18] I pray that the eyes of your heart may be enlightened in order that you may know the hope to which he has called you, the riches of his glorious inheritance in his holy people, [19] and his incomparably great power for us who believe."

By praying over the church in Ephesus, Paul is acting out his Levitical role as church leader. He is caring for the temple by praying blessing and promise over it and by giving thanks. He loves well by praying well.

I mentioned earlier that influence is built through relationship. Connecting with a congregation and praying for them will directly impact your leadership and how people respond to your leading in worship.

When a person knows you genuinely care for them and want to lead them well, they will recognize your genuine worship. But again, they need to know you. Part of connecting to someone is sharing your life with them. Transparency is key.

Transparency

Our world is moving more and more in the direction of transparency. People are seeking after something real. They are seeking after truth. For this reason, it is imperative that our leadership is transparent and authentic. If we are faking it, our congregation's will know. On the other side, when we are up front about who we are and still worship wholeheartedly, people see that too. When you are involved in a congregation and transparent with them in your thankfulness and praise, as well as your struggles, hardships, and pain, and continue to step onto a stage to joyfully praise the Father, you are pointing to Jesus.

One worship leader I know said this about transparency in worship:

"This lifetime is the only time in all of eternity that we will have the opportunity to worship, to praise God through hardship. In heaven, there will be no more pain, no more tears. No more hardship. This is the only time we have for that kind of praise. How sweet a sound must that be to God?"

Becoming a leader in transparency is key to leading effectively because transparency proves authenticity.

In 2 Corinthians 12:7-10, The Apostle Paul demonstrates transparency by describing his struggles to the church in Corinth.

"Therefore, in order to keep me from becoming conceited, I was given a thorn in my flesh, a messenger of Satan, to torment me. [8] Three times I pleaded with the Lord to take it away from me. [9] But he said to me, "My grace is sufficient for you, for my power is made perfect in weakness." Therefore, I will boast all the more gladly about my weaknesses, so that Christ's power may rest on me. [10] That is why, for Christ's sake, I delight in weaknesses, in insults, in hardships, in persecutions, in difficulties. For when I am weak, then I am strong."

Paul had committed his life to spreading the gospel, training leaders and planting churches; he was one of the biggest influences in the early church; yet, he still shared his struggles, his hardships, his persecutions and his difficulties with the Church. He didn't hide himself. Paul's hardships were real. Sharing them made him a better leader. Sharing struggles took him off of a pedestal and made him relatable. Transparency proved his love for Christ.

Be a Lead Worshiper

The Levites showed their love for God by caring for the temple, but that wasn't their only job. In 1 Chronicles 16:4, the Levites were instructed to to minister before the ark of the Lord, to extol, thank, and praise the Lord, the God of Israel. 1 Chronicles 23:30 says that they were to stand every morning to thank and praise the Lord. They were to do the same in the evening. Thankfulness and praise were key aspects of being a Levite.

Thankfulness is simply making yourself aware of blessing. This is an aspect of worship ministry that is often overlooked, even though we are often singing about and asking for God's blessing. As worship pastors, we should look for blessings and celebrate them. We should be training our teams to do the same and letting that spill over into our congregation's. Thankfulness, the awareness of blessing, leads to praise.

To praise is to express adoration to God. In 1 Chronicles 16:8-36 David directs the Levites in the manner in which they should praise God.

"8 Give praise to the Lord, proclaim his name; make known among the nations what he has done.
9 Sing to him, sing praise to him; tell of all his wonderful acts. 10 Glory in his holy name; let the

hearts of those who seek the Lord rejoice.[11] Look to the Lord and his strength; seek his face always.[12] Remember the wonders he has done, his miracles, and the judgments he pronounced, [13] you his servants, the descendants of Israel, his chosen ones, the children of Jacob.[14] He is the Lord our God; his judgments are in all the earth.[15] He remembers[c] his covenant forever, the promise he made, for a thousand generations,[16] the covenant he made with Abraham, the oath he swore to Isaac.[17] He confirmed it to Jacob as a decree, to Israel as an everlasting covenant: [18] "To you I will give the land of Canaan as the portion you will inherit." [19] When they were but few in number, few indeed, and strangers in it,[20] they wandered from nation to nation, from one kingdom to another.[21] He allowed no one to oppress them; for their sake he rebuked kings: [22] "Do not touch my anointed ones; do my prophets no harm." [23] Sing to the Lord, all the earth; proclaim his salvation day after day.[24] Declare his glory among the nations, his marvelous deeds among all peoples.[25] For great is the Lord and most worthy of praise; he is to be feared above all gods. [26] For all the gods of the nations are idols, but the Lord made the heavens.[27] Splendor and majesty are before him;

strength and joy are in his dwelling place. [28] Ascribe to the Lord, all you families of nations, ascribe to the Lord glory and strength.[29] Ascribe to the Lord the glory due his name; bring an offering and come before him. Worship the Lord in the splendor of his[c] holiness. [30] Tremble before him, all the earth! The world is firmly established; it cannot be moved.[31] Let the heavens rejoice, let the earth be glad; let them say among the nations, "The Lord reigns!" [32] Let the sea resound, and all that is in it; let the fields be jubilant, and everything in them! [33] Let the trees of the forest sing, let them sing for joy before the Lord, for he comes to judge the earth. [34] Give thanks to the Lord, for he is good; his love endures forever. [35] Cry out, "Save us, God our Savior; gather us and deliver us from the nations, that we may give thanks to your holy name, and glory in your praise." [36] Praise be to the Lord, the God of Israel, from everlasting to everlasting."

Here, David recalls specific blessings, specific promises, and he praises God for them. He declares that God is savior and Lord. David extols God. The word extol, used in verse 16:4, means to praise enthusiastically, or with passion. The Levites were instructed to praise God and to praise Him passionately. That's exactly what we should be training our worship teams to do. David gave the Levites a model. Then the Levites became the model. That is a great lesson for us, as modern day Levites, to learn: become the model.

Model Worship

Many worship pastors, leaders, and teams become frustrated with their congregations because they aren't worshiping, yet they fail to realize that their congregations may not know how. They need a model. We must become not only leaders of worship, but modelers of worship.

The idea of modeling worship is one that I talk with my team about often. Specifically, I speak mostly about expressive worship. This is important because many congregations will not go further than they are led. Most are not sure what they are allowed to do, so they mirror what they see on the stage. For this reason, expressive worship is essential to leading a worship service.

When a worship team raises their hands, prays in the Spirit or falls to their knees, it allows the congregation to do the same. If we are truly worshiping, our church will soon catch on.

Expressive worship teaches the congregation new

ways to worship and pushes them to a new level of intimacy with God. Although physical expression may not define worship, biblically speaking, it is a piece of it.

In Exodus 15, we see Moses singing in praise. In Psalm 134, the psalmist gives direction to lift your hands and bless the Lord. 2 Samuel 6 shows us David dancing with all his might. In Matthew 26, we find Jesus kneeling in prayer, and in Ephesians 6 we see Paul praying in the Spirit. If physical expression is an act of worship, we are to model it. It should be clear that worship leaders are worshiping.

I'm not the most out-going person in the world. I'm not the most expressive person in the world. I'm not even the most energetic person. But I know that when I step onto a stage to lead in worship, I have a responsibility to be all of these things. I am often seen jumping, lifting my hands or dropping to my knees. On stage, these actions are bigger and more obvious than they would be if I were in the congregation. That's because I am modeling expressive worship for my congregation. It's not a show, it's showing people how.

The Music

Lastly, as we look at the Levites, we find that they

prophesied with harps, lyres, and cymbals. They prophesied with music. Finally, we have gotten to music. But before I go on, I want to reiterate how important everything outside of music is. By leading well outside of music, by caring for the temple, we set ourselves up to lead well in the music, to lead well in worship. Outside of music is where we, as pastors, should pastor the most. It's where our worship team, our team of ministers, should minister the most. By caring for the temple, we are preparing hearts for worship.

As we step into corporate worship we are stepping into 1 Chronicles 25:6. Here, David instructs the Levites to prophesy, thank, and praise the Lord accompanied by harps, lyres, and cymbals in the House of God. Through worship, praise, and thankfulness, they were to prophesy. This translates to modern day through our set lists.

A worship set list should always ascribe worthiness, express adoration, and voice an awareness of blessing. In doing so, we declare the promises of God. It should also speak to what is being prayed in the heart of the church. This is where prophesy comes in. Through the songs that we sing, we connect the prayers of the church to the promises of God. The knowledge of a congregation's prayer should lead directly to the declaration of God's promise through the songs you lead.

When a set list is created out of the prayers of the church, the promises you are singing become prophesy you are proclaiming. This is why it is so important to stay connected to your church. When declaring God's promise over a specific prayer, you are both ministering to the needs of the congregation and facilitating the worship of God.

A person's worship becomes much more real when they are worshiping God for a promise that directly correlates with a prayer they are praying. Something comes to life in their spirit when they realize that God has already answered their prayer, that He has already promised it to them. When we declare promise in response to prayer, people learn of God's love. They learn who He is. That He has set them free, that He is the Healer, that He is the Giver of Life, that He is King.

Develop your team as Levites, get connected to your church and declare promise in response to prayer and your worship services will come alive.

What to Remember

Our biblical model, as worship leaders and pastors, is the Levites.

The Levites were charged with care of the temple, the building. We are charged with care of the temple, the people.

Connect with the church. Influence is built through relationship.

Love the church. The greatest measure of how well you are loving someone is how well you are praying for them.

Lead with transparency. Transparency proves authenticity.

Be a lead worshiper.

Model worship. Your congregation may not know how to worship.

Finding the Team
Chapter Four

I want to take a moment to talk about finding the worship team that you need. I do the majority of this through an extensive audition process. In all honesty, I have a love/hate relationship with auditions. I love finding new talent, growing my team and investing in new musicians and leaders. But I don't love the other side – weeding through the less talented, telling people no, and what sometimes feels like killing dreams. Auditions can be both exciting and difficult. Regardless of feelings though, they are necessary in order to build excellence.

The truth is, not everyone is qualified to serve in this capacity. I've led with some extremely talented individuals whose hearts just weren't there. I've also led with individuals who have incredible hearts for worship, but have no skill. As unfortunate as it is to turn people away, especially when you need musicians, it is sometimes necessary. Sometimes, churches get mixed up a little bit in the belief that everyone should serve. Although it is true that all followers of Jesus are called to ministry, all followers of Jesus are not called to the same ministry. They are not all called to your ministry. And some may be, but are not ready yet. Here, I want to discuss two areas that I believe are "must- haves" on a worship team.

Psalm 78:72 says, "and David shepherded them with integrity of heart. With skillful hands he led them."

My friend Kurtis often quotes this scripture and emphasizes that this concept is both/and, not either/or. David led with both integrity of heart and skillful hands. He led with both character and competency. Personally, I believe this is one of the most significant leadership ideas in all of the bible – both skill and integrity are necessities. In his book, *Next Generation Leader*, Andy Stanley (2003) says, "Your talent and giftedness as a leader have the potential to take you farther than your character can sustain you. That ought to scare you." (p. 151) What Andy Stanley is saying here is that neither talent nor character is enough on its own.

Before he was the Apostle Paul, Saul was extremely competent. He was knowledge-able, having trained under significant leaders of his day and he was very successful too. His character, however, suffered. We can all see that reading his story.

However, after God got ahold of him and knocked him off his horse, Paul spent time in the Father's presence. In doing so, he got a character boost. Now, 2000 years later, he is still influencing the world. He's still seen as a leader in the Church.

He got in the presence of God, stayed in the presence of God and let God mold his character.

If we want to be used by God, we can set ourselves up for that to happen by growing in heart and in hands - in character and in competency.

We'll simplify things a little bit by equating skillful hands, or competency, with music and integrity of heart, or character, with ministry. Those are the two "must-haves" we are looking at. Although we should constantly be teaching and training our teams, there needs to be some level of character and competency in place before joining. There are two reasons I say that: First, I don't have the time in my week to teach someone a new instrument or about the theology of worship. Secondly, I believe it is a biblical approach. 1 Chronicles 25:7 says that the Levites, our models for leading worship, were skilled and trained in music for the Lord.

Auditions

The first thing I'm looking for in the audition process

is the person's musical skill level. Music is the biggest tool that we use in worship ministry. It is important that this tool, as with any, is operated with skill. As we discussed in previous chapters, music accompanies prophesy, helps to declare promise and is an avenue for prayer. If we find value in these things, we should value the tools that support them.

As I said before, I use an extensive audition process to test skillfulness. The audition process consists of 4 phases. A potential team member must complete all 4 phases before joining our team. This may seem a little out the ordinary or even unnecessary, but it is the best process I have found so far. At times, I have shortened this process by a step or even lengthened it by a step, it is not a one size fits all program, but for the most part it stays the same.

Phase One

Phase one consists of an initial audition with myself and a worship leader on my team. I send the auditioning musician 2 songs a few days ahead of time. Along with the recording, I send them chord charts, the proper key, tempo, and the time signature of each song. Then I meet with them to hear them play. Usually, we play through each song twice, my assisting worship leader and I playing with them. Before the first time, I always tell the new musician that I'm not counting anything against them. I want any nerves to settle. The second time, I pay a little closer attention. After the music, we sit down to talk for a few minutes – kind of an informal interview. I'm not drilling them with questions here. I'm simply asking about their history as a musician, with the church, and with the Lord.

Phase Two

From there, if the musician passes, we move them onto phase two. In phase two the new musician joins the entire worship team for a midweek rehearsal. They will rehearse with or alongside a current member who plays their instrument or sings their part. This phase, and occasionally the next, are where I might lengthen the audition process a little bit. Having someone play with the band will sometimes show me things I didn't see in their initial audition, such as the way the way they play a part when doubled by another instrument or if they seek to be the loudest instrument on stage.

Phase 3

In phase 3 an auditioning musician will join me, and usually a stripped down band, for a Wednesday night service. At my current church, the Wednesday services are much smaller than on Sunday morning. This gives me an opportunity to see how a musician plays in front of the congregation as well as how they lead.

Phase 4

In phase 4 the auditioning musician joins the worship team for Sunday morning services. There are a few reasons this is important: it gives me another chance to see how they lead, this time with a larger crowd. It also shows me how they handle getting to the church early and playing in multiple services.

The first two phases deal mostly with competency in music. In the first two phases, while dealing with skill, I'm paying attention to how well they know their instrument and play with the band, how they stay on the click track, and how comfortable they are with the music.

Phases three and four of the audition process deal more with a person's leadership ability, character, and heart for ministry. I say that because I can see these things tested more in the later phases. It begins with the end of phase one though, in the informal interview. That is often my first glimpse into a person's heart for worship. It is also an opportunity for me to explain our mission and vision as a team. As I explain the mission and vision, I am looking for a response. Not a specific one per se, but I want to know that it is something they can get on board with. I want to know how the beliefs of an individual interested in leadership align with the beliefs of the church. From there, in phases three and four, I'm looking at how the new musician interacts with the team and with the congregation.

At one church I worked at, I held an audition for a lead guitar player, Joe. Joe was good guitar player, he just needed a little work adapting to our team. He wasn't used to playing with a band or to playing our style of music. That was an adjustment I could work with.

The problem came when he had made it past the first three phases. We were rehearsing for Sunday morning, Joe's phase 4, and he was not playing the proper guitar part for a song. When I instructed him on how to play the part, he rolled his eyes and mumbled something under his breath. Later, at the end of the rehearsal, Joe left. The problem here was that I hold a team meeting after every rehearsal. Things may have been different if Joe had told me he had a prior obligation that he needed to get to, but he didn't. When I said "hold on, we're going to meet for a minute," Joe shrugged and said he had to go. He didn't play that Sunday.

Now, maybe he was having a bad day or maybe I'm too hard on potential teammates, but I couldn't bring Joe on the team because of his attitude. After a conversation with another pastor on staff to make sure I was making the right move, I found out that Joe had been at the church a long time and had a little bit of an entitlement issue when it came to things he wanted to do. As I build a team, I'm looking to build a team of ministers. For that reason, it is of great importance that I have a team whose heart is aligned with the vision and can take direction in order to move that vision forward. It is important that musicians are humble and willing to be discipled.

What if they don't make it?

In the instance that someone does not make the team, I always try to encourage them in both their musical and ministerial endeavors. I send them an email thanking them for stepping out and auditioning to join the worship team. I want them to know that I truly do appreciate the effort and the interest. From there, I tell them I don't believe they are ready for the stage. There could be any number of reasons why I stopped the audition, but I always include three to four items to work on if they would like to audition again in the future. Often for vocalists, they need work with harmonies. Many times for musicians, they need work with the click track. Whatever the case, I try to point the musician or vocalist to a resource that can help them improve. At the end of the email, I always include Psalm 78:72 and talk about leading with both character and competency. Then, I thank them again and encourage them to move forward in finding where God wants to use their gifts.

Consecrated Hearts

Above all, when I'm looking for the team, I'm looking for those who have consecrated their hearts. 1 Chronicles 15:14 tells us the Levites consecrated themselves in preparation to carry the ark of the Lord. They consecrated themselves in order to step into the Father's presence. Consecration means to make something holy, to declare something as sacred. The temple was a sacred place. The ark, a symbol of God's presence, was a sacred place. The temple of the Holy Spirit, the believer, whose heart is where His presences rests, should be declared sacred. I'm searching for people to join my team who have made themselves holy, who have dedicated themselves to the Lord.

Joshua 3:5 says, "Consecrate yourselves, for tomorrow the Lord will do amazing things among you." Just before that, in Joshua 3:3, the Israelites are told to follow the ark, the presence of God. Just as the Israelites, we are to make ourselves holy and stay in the presence of God. There, He will do amazing things. I fully believe that if these are the people we are bringing into leadership on our teams, those who have consecrated themselves to God, He will do amazing things in our churches. Our churches will be more impactful, we will see more lives come to Jesus, and God will be glorified.

My last thought on finding the right team is this:

Become who you are searching for. Excellence attracts excellence. Consecration attracts consecration.

If you are searching for excellent musicians to join your team, you and your current team need to become excellent in the music that you are playing. That doesn't mean that you have to have award winning musicians. It just means finding out what you are good at and doing that to the best of your ability. Grow from there one step at a time.

If you are searching for consecrated hearts, you and your current team must consecrate your hearts. You need to commit to making yourself sacred. Those with consecrated hearts, who are looking to join a team, will not want to join a team who is not on the same page as they are. They want to see the amazing things God has promised them. They cannot do that with a team that is not consecrated.

You will serve yourself, your team, and your church well when you begin to strive for excellence in both heart and hands. Both character and competence are defining factors in leadership. Building a great team begins with learning to be a great leader. Pursue these factors and that is what you will become. When that is what you become, that is what you will attract.

What to Remember

David led with both skill of hand and integrity of heart. He led with character and competency. (see Psalm 78:72)

The Levites were skilled and trained in music for the Lord. (See 1 Chronicles 25:7)

As you build a team, look to build a team of ministers.

Worship musicians should always be humble and willing to be discipled.

Search for those who have consecrated their hearts to the Lord.

Become who you are searching for. Excellence attracts excellence. Consecration attracts consecration.

Following Your Leader
Chapter Five

One of the most important relationships you need to have as a worship pastor, I believe, is a healthy relationship with your lead pastor. Although there are many leaders in your church, and maybe even many pastors on staff, no one shares the stage or is in the spotlight as much as the lead pastor and the worship pastor. These two roles share the face and the voice of the church. They should be looking the same direction and speaking the same vision.

Typically, the lead pastor sets the vision for the church. As a worship pastor, you should be behind that vision, whether it is an ultimate goal, for a project, or for a sermon series. People will come to you for your thoughts on the subject. Those thoughts should align with that of the lead pastor.

This is the case in worship as well. Although you, as the worship pastor, may be the main vision caster for worship, your vision should come out of the same place as the lead pastor. If you're curious as to how to make that happen, it's easy. Just ask. Ask your lead pastor what he or she would like to see in worship services. The answer may be that they want you to come up with that. If that is the case, go for it. But if they have thoughts, listen intently to find the direction that you need to go, then voice that vision to your team.

The same thing can be said for the music that you are playing. In every church I have led worship at there have been complaints about the music. It's always too loud, too quiet, too old, or too new. It's never right. In many of these churches, the complaints haven't come to me, but to the lead pastor. What I've found is that these complaints are much easier to manage if there is a vision for the music. In many cases, I've explained the vision for the sound to the person complaining and the issue was dropped. What's important to note here is that if someone does not understand the vision, it's hard to get behind.

In one church I was leading at, an email came in telling us that the music was too loud. The person went on to tell us that God could hear quiet songs, that His goal is to hear our hearts. As true as that is, what the particular person wanted was not the style we were going for. I was fairly new to the church at the time, so I mentioned it to the lead pastor. He said this, "do you want it loud? I want it loud." And that was the end of the conversation. We had a vision for the sound that we wanted.

To some that may come off as harsh, but the truth is our musical vision lines up with our worship vision. Our worship vision lines up with the vision of our church. My lead pastor and I agreed that we cannot compromise vision for someone who just doesn't like it. That said, if my lead pastor would have asked me to change something, I would have.

The reason I would have changed the sound, or anything else, upon his request is simple. It's partly because he's my boss, but mostly because he's my leader. He's my pastor. I lead our church under his leadership. I pastor under him. I've placed myself under his authority and I, according to scripture, need to respect that authority. Even if I disagree.

Hebrews 13:17 says, "Have confidence in your leaders and submit to their authority, because they keep watch over you as those who must give an account. Do this so that their work will be a joy, not a burden, for that would be of no benefit to you."

Don't get me wrong, if you have a healthy relationship with your lead pastor, there should be some room for disagreement on how things are done. As long as it is in private. There should be conversation. However, by the time you leave the privacy of the room where that conversation is taking place, you should be on board with whatever has been decided. If not, you risk growing bitter and losing a piece of the relationship you have. Honor your pastor by following his lead. This is especially important if you are in front of the church. You are a team. Honor your pastor at all times.

One day at lunch, a pastor I was working under and I had a disagreement about a concept. We ended up talking about it off and on the rest of the day. At one point, I said something that was a little out of line. It wasn't the point I was making that was off base, it was the way in which I phrased it. I said something that was unintentionally disrespectful. If that wasn't enough already, I said it in front of someone else too.

The next day, I knocked on his door and apologized. He shrugged it off like it was nothing and even laughed a little bit. Because it was nothing. The concept we were discussing was not of major importance. It actually had nothing to do with anything church related. He completely understood. After I apologized, that was it. Afterward though, I made myself more aware of who is around when I'm speaking. He never asked me to do that, but it was something I could do to honor him.

I don't say that because the lead pastor should be put on a pedestal. I am far from believing that should be the case. I say that because you are leading a church together. You are ministering to people together. You are growing the kingdom together. If something comes between you, you will be less effective. If your relationship suffers, the church will in turn suffer.

Prioritizing Relationship

Worship pastors should prioritize their relationship with their lead pastor. There are two ways that I recommend doing this. First, make a point to spend time together. Whether it is in the office, going to lunch, or grabbing coffee, find some time for the two of you to hang out. Do this periodically. I've found that it can beneficial to small talk and just to shoot the breeze for a little while. Talk about life. After that, talk about what's happening in the church and what you're doing to achieve the vision. Be sure to note, this shouldn't be like a quarterly review. It's just a chance to stay connected regarding what God has called you to do together.

Second, pray for your lead pastor. This probably should go without saying, but think about it. When was the last time you actually prayed for your pastor? It's important to do so. And to do it often.

1 Timothy 2:1-2 says, "I urge, then, first of all, that petitions, prayers, intercession and thanksgiving be made for all people— for kings and all those in

authority, that we may live peaceful and quiet lives in all godliness and holiness." It goes on to say that this is pleasing to the lord.

1 Timothy 5:17 says, "the elders who direct the affairs of the church well are worthy of double honor, especially those whose work is preaching and teaching."

Honor your pastor well by praying for him well. In Colossians 1:9-12, Paul prays over the church, asking God to give them knowledge, wisdom, and understanding, that they would bear fruit and be strengthened. What Paul prays here is exactly what we should be praying for our pastors.

Colossians 1:9-12 says, "For this reason, since the day we heard about you, we have not stopped praying for you. We continually ask God to fill you with the knowledge of his will through all the wisdom and understanding that the Spirit gives, so that you may live a life worthy of the Lord and please him in every way: bearing fruit in every good work, growing in the knowledge of God, being strengthened with all power according to his glorious might so that you may have great endurance and patience, and giving joyful thanks to the Father, who has qualified to share in the inheritance of his holy people in the kingdom of light."

I don't know about you, but I want my leader leading

out of a place of knowledge of God's will. I want him leading out of place of wisdom and understanding, beckoned by the Holy Spirit. I want him to bear fruit. I want him to have endurance and patience and joy. On a more selfish level, those things are going to make a great work environment. On a more serious level, those things are going to grow the Kingdom of Heaven. Those things are going to push the Great Commission forward. Those things will fill his spirit and be poured out into everyone under him. Those things will be poured into you.

I can't stress enough how important this relationship is. Always be connected with your lead pastor. When I first stepped into my current position, I had a long conversation with my pastor about this very idea. In fact, he brought it up first. That's how important it is to him. Because he recognizes that importance, it makes me want to work with him even more. His prioritizing of our relationship built my trust and showed his heart for those he leads. The result of this relationship has been personal growth in me. I've become a better pastor because I've worked to build a solid relationship with my pastor.

On the other hand, in my time in ministry I've heard a lot of complaints about leadership. And honestly, I've probably complained myself. Many times I have heard that a lead pastor is disagreeable, unfriendly, or even mean. What's sad is most of the people making that statement loved their lead pastor in the beginning. But something changed. Over time a bitterness grew out of something. Maybe the pastor isn't forward thinking enough, maybe he's too careful, maybe he's too strict —there are numerous possibilities. In the past when someone told me that, I would respond with "man, that's tough. I'm so sorry." Now, I respond with, "What are you doing to prioritize that relationship? What are you doing to honor your pastor?" As with any relationship, when you make it a priority it will grow.

Hebrews 10:24-25 says, " [24]And let us consider how we may spur one another on toward love and good deeds, [25] not giving up meeting together, as some are in the habit of doing, but encouraging one another—and all the more as you see the Day approaching."

This is the verse that I try to have in mind at all times when considering my relationship with my lead pastor, or anyone on our staff. I want my time working with this team, whether it's a few years or the rest of my life, to be a time of encouraging them in love.

The Message version of the bible says *"let's see how inventive we can be in encouraging love and helping out."* I love the way this is phrased: "let's see how inventive we can be." It asks more of me than to give a compliment. It urges me to think of new ways to encourage, new ways minister, new ways lead well. It's been said that leading well is following well. My desire is to be the best follower of my pastor that I can be. I believe that doing so will make me a better leader. I believe it will make me a better pastor.

<u>What to Remember</u>

As a worship pastor, one of the most important relationship you can have is a healthy relationship with your lead pastor.

The lead pastor and the worship pastor should always be looking the same direction and speaking the same vision.

Honor your pastor at all times.

If this relationship suffers, the church will suffer.

Pray Colossians 1:9-12 over your pastor.

Preparing to Lead
Chapter Six

So, it's almost time to lead a service. You've spent the week discipling worship leaders, developing the team, and casting vision for worship, but outside of that, how do you properly prepare for service? In my experience, most worship pastors don't give this enough thought. I haven't always. Many of us have been doing this for years and leading worship has just become part of the routine, part of the job. A lot of us thought we only needed work on the other stuff: the vision casting and discipleship side of things. Many of us started out with the Sunday morning experience. Somebody asked us to lead, so we rehearsed with the team and just jumped up and led when Sunday came around. There wasn't a lot of preparation to it. We thought we were solid musicians; we didn't need it.

This can be both good and bad. The good part is that

it usually means a worship pastor is comfortable on stage, comfortable with the job. Some level of comfort is extremely beneficial in leading well. The bad part is often times we don't improve our leading because we aren't evaluating how we are doing it. Often, we settle for good because we aren't preparing for great. Excellence comes by way of evaluation. The challenge I want to propose in this chapter is to evaluate how you are preparing to lead. Here, I'll show you some things that I do to prepare, both practically and spiritually, and how they help me pastor my congregation.

Just as I mentioned when discussing the Levites, I always start with my congregation. I am looking at what their needs are. To get a glimpse of this, I often try to connect with my lead pastor regarding the sermon series or the particular sermon he is preaching. I look at what my pastor is trying to convey and how I can help him achieve that through our time in worship. Often, even just doing this one thing gets me out of the week in/week out routine of the job of leading worship and helps to me to focus on the opportunity I have to minister. It helps to choose songs that actually make a difference instead of choosing songs that are fun to play and "work." It helps me to remember that Sunday morning is the biggest outreach, the biggest opportunity for ministry that we have all week. That's not something to take lightly. Once I know the needs, the subjects I need to minister on, I can start building a set list.

Set Lists

As I said before, I want my set lists to connect the prayers of the church to the promises of God, but I do want to note that this connection happens in different ways. And often in sort of waves. Allow me to explain. I split worship songs into different categories based upon their purpose. Having a clear purpose in mind for a song tells you where to put it in the set. It tells you how to use it. The four categories that I use are as follows: Invitation, Declaration, Response, and Encounter.

Songs of Invitation

Songs of invitation do just what the title says. They invite. But they don't invite God into a service, as you might think. They are not "you're welcome here" songs. Invitation songs invite people in. They are inviting people to worship. I think we, as worshippers, often forget that everyone isn't always ready for worship. Everyone hasn't been up since 5 am so they could be at church early for a rehearsal and then for a service. Everyone isn't a worship leader. Most people need some time to prepare their hearts, to remember why they are there. People need to be invited in.

In my current church, we have a lot of young families, 30 somethings with kids. That's our largest demographic, so I have to recognize on Sunday morning that some of my congregation was up at 5 am, but not because they wanted to be. They were up because they had to change diapers or calm a crying toddler. Sometimes they had to skip breakfast, or had to change their kids clothes three times, or they haven't had coffee. Sometimes the "victory" in their life is just getting there in the first place. With all of that going on, it may take a few minutes for them to be ready for worship. So I have to gently invite them in.

Invitation songs aren't usually what you think of when people are weeping at the altar. Invitation songs are usually the fast, fun songs. They're praising God, they're worshipful, but your goal here isn't necessarily life change. Your goal is to say, "You made it. Lay your burdens down and worship a God who loves you."

Songs of Declaration

Declaration songs are songs that declare who God is. This is where we begin to look at the "prayers to promise" idea. They declare the names of God and the promises associated with those names. They declare that He is good, that He is victorious, that He is King, that He is Savior and more. Declaration songs are reminders or even sometimes teachers of the character of God.

When I am choosing a declaration song I am choosing a song that declares a promise or a name of God that directly relates to the prayers being prayed in my church. If I know that healing is largely being prayed for in my church, I am going to lead songs that declare that God is the healer or songs that tell a story of healing, like a song based out of John 9 where Jesus heals the blind.

The same goes if I know there is victory being prayed for in my church, whether it is over addiction, disease, relationships, or anything else. I am going to lead songs that declare that God is victorious, that He reigns as King, and that He has it under control.

The declaration of God's promise should always lead to a response. Response songs are often the "third song" in worship. They're the slower, deeper, more powerful ones. They're the ones that you may riff on for a while and really try to pull people in. Response songs are often the "I love you" songs. In a response song you are pointing to God in a new way. These songs are more likely to talk about worshiping on bended knee, or coming to the altar, or telling God that He is worthy, that you'll praise Him as long as you live, etc.

When I am leading a declaration song I am declaring God's promise, speaking of His blessings. In a response song I am thanking God for the blessing. The recognition of God's blessing should immediately result in our responding in worship. The worship pastor's job in a song of response is to be a leader in thankfulness, a leader in telling Him that He is worthy, a leader in giving Him glory for all that He is, all that He has done, and all that He will do.

Songs of Encounter

That last category I want to talk about is songs of encounter. These are my, and most worship leader's I know, favorite songs. These songs tend to start out really ambient then get big and powerful and then drop back down. These are our most dynamic songs musically. On the spiritual side, these songs often talk about God's presence. They are songs we're singing when we want nothing more than to see the power of God, to see God move in our services, in our lives, and in our communities. These are the songs we are often singing when we are deep in prayer and are searching for His voice.

Personally, when I lead songs of encounter, I am always thinking of altars. I don't necessarily mean the front of the stage or anything like that. Just a place of worship. All over the Old Testament, God tells His people to build altars. The Israelites built and altar where God parted the Jordan. Samuel built an altar where God defeated the Philistines. Jacob built an altar where God revealed himself in a dream. These altars were places where God's people could go back to and remember His faithfulness, love, and mercy, and worship Him for that.

The songs that I lead during times of encounter are often like musical altars in the hearts of my congregation. Sometimes they are songs we happened to be singing when God moved in the past. When that's the case, people are going back to the altar to worship. Sometimes they are songs that have a great impact because of what God is doing in the service that day, like bringing healing or victory. In those times we are building a new altar together.

An altar is a place of encounter. An altar is a powerful place of worship. Altars are a symbol of a new beginning. And they are a tool that God uses to keep us from forgetting what He wants us to remember.

Prepare for a service well by thoughtfully choosing the set list. Remember that as worship pastor's we aren't just choosing songs; we're choosing the avenue's through which we are ministering. Thoughtfully choosing a set and doing so by category gives vision for each song and for your service.

I think many of us, as worship pastors, want our congregations to always be ready for an encounter, but to our disappointment, that isn't the case. We can't always start there. Our congregations aren't ready. We have to be ok with that. The truth is, as exciting as the encountering God aspect of a worship service is, it's not the only part that matters. We should first recognize God and his promises and praise and worship Him.

Though we can't always start with encounter, we don't always have to start with invitation. Depending on the type of service, we may start in another place, like with a song of declaration. If I'm walking into a conference to lead worship, I likely will not start in the same place that I do on Sunday morning. Walking into a conference, I am more likely stepping on stage in front of people who are expecting God to move. They may have bought tickets or cleared their schedule to be there. They expect to be in a different place than in a typical Sunday morning service because it is outside of a week to week routine. Also, a conference is typically set up to be more of a believer service. There are fewer unchurched people there. Conferences are often a time for believers to recharge. When that is the case I'm more likely to start with declaration, move to invitation, and then spend time on encounter.

Similarly, on Wednesday nights at my current church, I don't always have to start with invitation. I can move right into declaration or even response. The difference here is that I know who is in that service. I know that Wednesday services are usually full of people seeking to learn more of God. They are full of worshippers.

In my preparation time, I am always looking at the type of service I am stepping into. From there, I look at my congregation, what they need to learn, are praying for or are celebrating, and then I choose songs based on where I believe I need to start and end. I am taking people on a sort of journey with these songs. Because of that, I often spend time in prayer over the specific songs. I ask God to work through the particular songs as my congregation worships.

For songs of invitation, I pray that God would begin to make himself known, that He would help people to turn their focus completely to Him, and that He would be glorified. For songs of declaration I first praise God for who He is and the promises we are declaring, I then pray that He would make Himself and that promise obvious to my congregation. When praying over songs of response, I pray that His goodness and glory would be known. That those singing would understand who they are worshiping. When I pray over songs of encounter, I ask that God would show up in people's lives, that he would move like never before in the hearts of my congregation, that His glory would be revealed, that His Spirit would cover the room and that no one would walk out without recognizing the presence of the Almighty God. Through all of this I pray my congregation would realize the importance of worship, the relational character of God, and would more clearly know His voice.

Prepare to Pastor

As important as knowing your congregation, connecting with your pastor, and preparing songs are for the worship pastor, it is just as important to prepare yourself to pastor. Most worship pastors spend most of their preparation time in rehearsal, but there is much more to it. Although preparing our hands is important, we also need to prepare our hearts and minds.

Prepare your heart through prayer. If you're praying over the songs you lead, you've already started this. My lead pastor asks me nearly every week if I am "prayed up." He wants to ensure that I am constantly praying and ready to minister. Even when I interviewed for my current position, he asked me about the importance of prayer in what I do. He explained that our church does not always stick to the script, that sometimes we would vary from the order of service. He needed to know that I could handle that and lead well in any circumstance. My answer to his question is what allows us to have complete trust in each other during a service. Our mutual pursuit of prayer has put our hearts in sync with God's heart for our church.

Walk into services prayerfully. Align your heart with God and with your leadership. Doing so will bring clarity to the vision for each service, it will build your leadership's trust in you and it will serve you well in your ministry.

In regards to your mind, prepare it by releasing everything to God. This isn't to say that you should fake it or act like you have everything together, but that you should realize what you have in Christ.

Colossians 3:1-17 says this:

"¹Since, then, you have been raised with Christ, set your hearts on things above, where Christ is, seated at the right hand of God. ² Set your minds on things above, not on earthly things. ³ For you died, and your life is now hidden with Christ in God. ⁴ When Christ, who is your life, appears, then you also will appear with him in glory.

⁵ Put to death, therefore, whatever belongs to your earthly nature: sexual immorality, impurity, lust, evil desires and greed, which is idolatry. ⁶ Because of these, the wrath of God is coming.ᴵ ⁷ You used to walk in these ways, in the life you once lived. ⁸ But now you must also rid yourselves of all such things as

these: anger, rage, malice, slander, and filthy language from your lips. ⁹ Do not lie to each other, since you have taken off your old self with its practices ¹⁰ and have put on the new self, which is being renewed in knowledge in the image of its Creator. ¹¹ Here there is no Gentile or Jew, circumcised or uncircumcised, barbarian, Scythian, slave or free, but Christ is all, and is in all.

¹² Therefore, as God's chosen people, holy and dearly loved, clothe yourselves with compassion, kindness, humility, gentleness and patience. ¹³ Bear with each other and forgive one another if any of you has a grievance against someone. Forgive as the Lord forgave you. ¹⁴ And over all these virtues put on love, which binds them all together in perfect unity.

¹⁵ Let the peace of Christ rule in your hearts, since as members of one body you were called to peace. And be thankful. ¹⁶ Let the message of Christ dwell among you richly as you teach and admonish one another with all wisdom through psalms, hymns, and songs from the Spirit, singing to God with gratitude in your hearts. ¹⁷ And whatever you do, whether in word or deed, do it all in the name of the Lord Jesus, giving thanks to God the Father through him."

We are aiming for verses 16 and 17, but verses 1 through 15 are how we get there. By handing everything over to God, we set ourselves up to be used by God. I am a more effective minister when I am not bogged down by life. My guess is that you will be too.

My last thought, when it comes to preparing to lead, is this: worship before you get on stage. Take the songs that you have already prepared and spend time in worship with them. Spend time singing them, praying them, and reading the scripture's the songs are written out of. Spend time with God. Doing so will both build your faith and your leadership. You'll realize the importance of different lyrics, you may find talking points, you may find something new to pray over your congregation or even your own life. The stage should not be the worship pastor's only place of worship. All pastors should find time to worship outside of Sunday morning. You have to be filled up in order to pour out.

The stage calls for a different kind of worship. The stage is not the place for the worship pastor to get lost in worship. It's a place for the worship pastor to lead in worship. On stage, you should be worshiping, but it is in a different way than the congregation worships. The worship pastor's role is kind of a point of connection between the needs of the church and the leading of the Holy Spirit. The worship pastor should hear from God on behalf of the church and lead in the church's response to God. It's a dual role. By being a point of connection, you are ministering to people. By leading the response, you are ministering to God. For that reason, you need to be aware. You need to be worshipped up, prayed up, and able to recognize the voice of God.

<u>What to Remember</u>

Know the needs of your congregation.

Become a connection point between the prayers of the church and the promises of God.

Have clear purposes for the songs that you lead.

Create musical altars in the hearts of your congregation.

Remember, you're not just choosing songs. You are choosing the avenues by which you are ministering.

Although preparing our hands is important, don't neglect to prepare your heart and your mind.

Worship before you get on stage.

Pastoring in a Service
Chapter Seven

Awareness of the room is often the first topic I bring up when it comes to leading a service. In order to be completely effective in ministry, the worship pastor should be completely aware of those he is ministering to. This starts in your preparation time with knowing the songs, their purposes, and being well rehearsed.

From there, the first thing to keep in mind is keeping your eyes open. Literally. Keeping your eyes open is something many new leaders often overlook and many seasoned leaders don't stop to think about. It may be a sort of nervousness or stage fright, but that nervousness needs to be overcome. Your effectiveness in leading worship will wane if you cannot see what is going on around you. There are three things that I am looking for during a service: engagement, reaction, and connection.

When looking for these items, it is important to remember the purpose of each song and the category it is in. You may be looking for something different out of each song. Invitation songs may not require much. Declaration songs should call for some engagement, and even more so with songs of response and encounter. There should be some level of engagement or reaction within these.

Engagement

Let's start with engagement. It's likely that everyone reading this has a different idea as to what engagement is. That's okay. Different congregations have different definitions of engagement in worship. What's important is that you do indeed have an idea of what it means for your congregation. Engagement needs to be defined.

For my congregation, when I am looking for engagement, I am looking for people singing, hands lifted, people kneeling, and people worshiping at the altar. During songs of invitation or declaration, I am more likely hearing voices and seeing hands raised. During songs of response and encounter, I am more likely to see kneeling and people moving toward the altar.

For other congregations I have led, engagement was

defined only by congregants singing, or even congregants simply standing in silence, focused on God. Whatever the case, engagement should be defined. It should also be modeled and taught. Look back at the Levites chapter for ideas on modeling worship. Stay tuned for ideas on teaching.

Reaction

When I talk about reaction I am moving away from singing and toward speaking. I am looking for how people are reacting to the words that I say on stage, between songs, in down moments, or anywhere else. I nearly always advise those leading worship, if they are going to speak, to direct the congregation to do something, to take action. This may sound like asking them to sing a new song to the Lord, meaning singing out their personal praises outside of the song. It may be urging them to lift their hands or kneel before God. It may simply be telling them to close their eyes and focus on the love of God.

I do this because I want my congregation to take on a new posture in worship. The hope is that this will move them into a new place of a worship, a fresh revelation of God, a new way to experience their Creator. As much I want my congregation to develop a habit of worship, I don't want them to develop a habit of going through the motions. I want them to do something new in order to experience something new.

How my congregation reacts to these statements tells me a lot. If there is no reaction, they may not be engaged or I may need to explain myself more thoroughly. I may need to teach more. If there is a reaction, I need to follow up some of my congregation to find out how they experienced God in that moment, if it was beneficial, or if they did it just because the guy with the microphone told them to. Reaction tells me a lot about how I am leading and where I need to lead in the future.

Connection

Lastly, I am looking for connection. Here, I am moving back to the songs I am leading. Throughout my entire set, whether it is three songs or ten, I am paying close attention to how my congregation is connecting to particular songs or even parts of songs. I gauge this by the amount of engagement in the song. I gauge this by how people seem to be worshiping.

Sometimes in worship, a song or a piece of one, will hit the nail on the head spiritually. There is a lyric or a thought that connects more than any other. As I am ministering in worship, I will often go back to that part and repeat it a few times. This is easier to gauge when you know the prayers of the church. Knowing those prayers gives insight ahead of time into what the most important parts of a song may be. If victory is being prayed for in my church, I know ahead of time that a line that connects may be "You are victorious!" So I'll plan to go back to that line. I'll give opportunity for congregants to focus on that particular promise of God.

I'm more likely to be looking for connection during songs of response and songs of encounter. Obviously, if you look at the "victory" example above, there are times in songs of declaration and probably even in songs of invitation that the congregation will connect with a piece of a song. However, waiting to go back into a lyric or a prayer until you reach a song of response or encounter will pull more people into worship, more people that need to spend time in focused worship.

Watching for connection is also important when something is being prayed for in a service as a body. I realize that could be a little confusing, as we have been talking about the prayers of the church for so long, but here I am moving away from personal prayers and toward corporate prayers of the entire body. For instance, sometimes in my church, we will pray for healing for one person as a body. When this is the case, I need to find a song or a part of a song that connects with that prayer. One of my worship leaders, Damaris, demonstrated this well in a recent service.

Toward the end of our worship service, one of our pastors led the congregation in a prayer of healing for a young girl who has had problems walking for the majority of her life. While our pastor was praying, Damaris cued the band to soften the music. As we moved toward the end of the prayer and the congregation began to celebrate all that God was doing and will do, Damaris led the team to build up the song. She knew to do this because she was aware of the room and aware of what was happening spiritually. She knew that it was her job to take the focus away from the band and put it onto prayer.

What made this moment, and Damaris' leadership, even more powerful was what she did while our pastor was praying. Damaris chose a portion of the song, which was written out of scripture and had to do with healing, to riff on. The song, in a very real way, became the prayer our church was praying and the prophesy our church was receiving. Through this song she connected the prayers of the church to the promises of God. As we began to celebrate, Damaris led us into another portion of the song, a portion that thanked God, a celebratory portion.

She couldn't have done this if she wasn't aware of the room. Damaris ministered well because she was aware of how the Spirit of God was moving and how the heart of our congregation was responding.

Spontaneous Worship

This brings me to the idea of spontaneous worship or flow. We've touched on it a little bit, but I want to talk about an effective way to ready yourself and your team for these moments. Flow can most easily be explained as a time of worship with no agenda. Often times, music is playing but no particular song is being sung and there isn't a rush for the band to get off stage. Flow is simply a series of worshipful moments.

This time in a service is often between songs or at the end of a set, but really, it could be anywhere. Flow can be seen as spontaneous or spirit led. Like anything else, flow can be too long, too short, or just right.

Worship leaders, typically either love or hate this time in a service. Some try to force it and some try to avoid it. Neither are great attitudes. The use of flow should be based on what a congregation needs and where the Spirit leads. As in any part of worship, it shouldn't be selfish or showy.

Major artists seem to make this look easy, and the truth is, it is. These artists aren't necessarily more anointed, better musicians, or better worship leaders.

The secret to it is planning. The best way to ready yourself for spontaneity is to rehearse it. If you're looking back at the term "spirit led" from above, don't think this is a contradiction. We make plans for all kinds of things that we expect God to do in a service. We build in times for altar calls, for sermons and for prayer. Worship should be no different.

When coming out of a song into a flow moment, have the particular chord progression or part of the song you are going into planned and communicated to the band. Let the band know if they will need to build the music or drop out. Come up with body language to communicate this in the moment. As I said before, knowing the prayers of the church gives insight into what piece of the song I may go back to. That is mostly likely the part that will be rehearsed.

In some cases, you may sing something different altogether, like a prayer or just simple phrase praising God. Doing so can be a great tool for changing the atmosphere of a service. There are two things to remember if you are singing a lyric or prayer that is not part of the song. First, be sure that the melody is easily attainable. It should be sing-able by those who are not professional singers. Second, be sure that this lyric or prayer is relatable. It should be a phrase that the congregation can catch onto and get behind. These words should point the congregation to Jesus. They should be words that spur your congregation on in worship.

In many moments of spontaneous worship, I have moved into a new song completely. I've learned to do two things to prepare for this as well. First, I have cues both vocally and with body language that tells the band I am changing direction and moving into a new song. The team should be well aware of and well-rehearsed in your signals to build up, drop out, or repeat. Second, when possible, I rehearse the song with the team. Sometimes, I'll know that if the moment calls for it, I will go into a particular song. If I know the song ahead of time, I rehearse it with the team. From there, I instruct them to wait for my cues before going into it.

If these areas are covered, there will be no problem. When flow is planned well, it is easily navigated. Proper planning allows the leader to trust the band so he or she can focus on where to lead and what the Spirit is saying.

Gatekeepers

Throughout the entire service, as I am watching for engagement, reaction, and connection and as I am speaking, singing prayers, or in spontaneous moments, I am looking to what I call Gatekeepers. 1 Chronicles 26 tells us of groups of Levites who were appointed to be gatekeepers of the temple. These Levites monitored the activities of the temple.

In a similar fashion, the gatekeepers that I have placed in my congregation monitor the activities of worship. They provide a gauge for me to know how the congregation is connecting to a song, a particular part of a song, or a word. I am looking for how the gatekeeper is engaged. If the gatekeeper is not engaged with the activities of the temple, something is wrong, and I likely either need to speak into it or move on.

These gatekeepers are often members of the worship team who are not on stage, leaders in the church, or other pastors. Gatekeepers are people that are both mature in the faith and have an active lifestyle of worship. It is important for gatekeepers to be mature in faith and active in worship because I need to know that they have an understanding of worship, that they are a proper gauge.

I cannot properly gauge the entire church on an individual who is weeping at the altar every week. That person likely hasn't matured in faith yet. I cannot gauge the entire church on someone who is overly excited and jumps and sings no matter what. That person is the same week to week. I can gauge the entire church on someone who has matured in faith and has a sensitivity to the Spirit of God.

Awareness of the Spirit

As we talk about awareness, I feel we must at least touch on awareness of the Spirit, or hearing from God as you lead. The reason I say we should touch on this is not because I feel it is less important. It is because if you are doing the other things we've discussed, I believe, you're already hearing from God. Some may disagree, but let me explain. Hopefully, I can demystify some of this subject when it comes to leading worship.

First, you should be hearing from God as you prepare for and pray over your worship set and services. I believe whole heartedly that if you are going the extra mile to find the prayers of your church and connecting them with the promises of God, you are already hearing from Him. One way that God speaks is through His Word. If you know His Word in such a way that allows you to communicate His promises, you have heard from Him.

Second, I believe you are hearing from God when you are aware of your congregation's engagement and connection in worship, when you are connected with gatekeepers. One way that God speaks is through His people. This is another reason why it is important to that gatekeepers are mature in faith and sensitive to the Sprit. What gatekeepers tell you about what is happening in the church can give direction to where the Spirit of God is leading.

The third item, when it comes to awareness of the Spirit, is discernment. Discernment comes into play in both of the points above as well as in speaking between songs, what to say, and praying over the congregation.

As you are preparing and praying, as you are leading songs, and as you are taking cues from the congregation and gatekeepers, it is your job, as the worship pastor, to discern what to do with that information. Sometimes, I don't need to go back to a part. Sometimes, I do. Sometimes, I need to end and cue my pastor to come up. Sometimes, I need my pastor to tell me to keep going. Sometimes, I don't need to speak. Sometimes, I do. Learning what to do and when is a matter of practicing discernment.

When starting out, connect with your lead pastor about it. Ask questions like, "do you think that was the right move? Why?" Let him know ahead of time that discernment on the stage is something you are practicing. Let him help you to grow. If you are connected to your lead pastor, as we discussed before, this should come more easily. You will both gain a sense of what needs to happen where.

In my experience, the place that discernment needs the most practice with worship pastors is in speaking between songs. In most cases, it isn't that speaking between songs is the wrong decision, it is that what is being said is ill-prepared. A worship pastor is speaking because the time feels right instead of speaking because they have something, or God has something, so to say. Many times, worship pastors will ramble, repeat, or 'um' their way through a speaking part. Doing so does no good and can end up being a distraction to worship. You need to have something to say.

What to Say

The words you speak over a congregation can set the tone for a service and push people to worship or they can interrupt it. Be very careful of how you are speaking over the congregation and the timing in which you do so. Whatever you say, be sure that it is backed up clearly by scripture. Practice this. As with anything else, speaking times should be prepared. If between songs, keep it short and simple. Make your point and move into the next song.

Often, worship pastors struggle with this. They don't prepare what they are going to say because they feel that it will be less genuine in the moment. If that's you, remember that just like with spontaneous moments, we prepare every other part of the service. We rehearse songs, write and practice sermons, we carve out time for prayer, and we set aside space for communion. Speaking opportunities between songs are no different.

A friend of mine once told me the story of two pastors, Steve and Tim, who were discussing sermon preparation. The first pastor, Steve, had every Sunday sermon prepared at least a week in advance. The second, Tim, waited until Sunday morning to start preparing. When Steve asked him his reasoning for this, Tim said that he didn't want to move faster than God. He wanted to wait and see what the Holy Spirit would say to him on Sunday morning. Steve responded by saying, "Well, if you ask God on Monday, He might just tell you on Monday."

Tim wasn't necessarily wrong in his approach, but his sermons were off the cuff and often unclear. Steve understood that a lack of preparation can hinder your ability to communicate clearly and in turn hinder your ability to minister effectively.

When I first started speaking between songs, I was terrible. It was not well planned, it was awkward and I rambled on and on. My thoughts were not organized. I was a distraction to worship instead of being a catalyst for it. When I realized that, it made me want to give up on public speaking altogether. I stopped for a long time. When I finally tried again, I knew I had to prepare. I started out by simply stating the scripture that song was written out of.

I realized that I could never go wrong speaking scripture over my congregation. Speaking scripture will give you a new confidence. Scripture taught me to speak with authority. If your words are based in scripture, you can be sure they are true and a word from God.

In the previous chapter, I talked about reading the scriptures your songs are written out of. Use them to find the words you are going to speak over your congregation. Talk about the promises you are praying over your church. Point people to God as the hero of their story. Let Him do the rest.

What to Remember

Keep your eyes open.

Define engagement for your congregation.

Be aware of what part of the song your congregation is connecting with.

Prepare for spontaneity.

Have gatekeepers in your services.

Prepare for opportunities to speak to your congregation in worship.

Teaching in Worship
Chapter Eight

In previous chapters, I've discussed modeling worship for a congregation and I've touched on speaking moments for the worship pastor. In this chapter, I want to talk about where those moments collide. I want to talk about teaching on and in worship. This is a subject that I think has been neglected in sense by worship pastors.

Many of us have waited and waited for a sermon series to teach on the subject, or worse, we have waited for congregants to just get it. Too often we have operated under the assumption that people already know or will pick it up from those around them. The truth though, is that many of our congregation don't know how to worship, often they don't really know what it is. They may understand that they are singing to God, but they often don't understand why or sometimes even what they are singing. When they do, however, spiritual growth seems to skyrocket, spiritual maturity seems to rise, and the expectancy of God to move tends to be great. I believe leaders of worship, pastors of worship, ought to be teachers of worship.

In this chapter, I want to talk a little bit about the importance of worship and how worship pastors can convey that to their congregations. I'll touch on what worship is, why we worship, and how we worship. I'll talk briefly on the actions of worship, the attributes of God, and the many names of God.

The hope here is not to teach you, the pastor, about these items as much as it is to give you ideas about what to teach and how to teach it. For that reason, I'll refrain from delving too deep into any one subject. Most of the teaching I do is done quickly, before a worship set or between songs, so that's how you should read this, as quick bits of information.

What is Worship

Three to four times a year I will take a moment to define worship for my congregation and talk briefly about why we worship. This is how it usually goes:

"Worship is defined as ascribing worth to God. It means to show reverence and adoration, a deep respect and a deep love, for God. Worship is where we tell God we love Him. It is where we stand in awe of Him, as John did in the Throne Room in Revelation 4. And it is where we surrender our lives to the King. It is a huge part of our relationship with Jesus.

Worship is, and always should be, for God, giving glory where glory is due. But one of the wonderful things about God is nothing we do ever stops with Him. He always points it back toward us. When we lift blessing up toward God, He rains blessing down on His people. Worship reminds us who we are. It reminds us whose we are. As a child of God, worship cannot be overlooked. It cannot be forgotten about. We worship God for who He is, what He has done, and what He will do."

What I said above is fairly simplistic, and possibly even a little cliché, but I believe it is important to begin with a base line, something even the newest believer can understand.

Why We Worship

At this point, I usually take a moment to dive into a name or an attribute of God. That's where it tends to go a little deeper. The names and attributes of God speak to why we worship. I talk about names and attributes when I am teaching briefly on worship, before going into music. I'll also talk about names and attributes between songs. Usually, when it's between songs, I am talking about a name or attribute we have just sang about or are about to sing about, a promise associated with the prayers of my church.

Attributes of God

Continuing from above, sometimes I'll talk about who God is:

"We worship God for who He is, what He has done, and what He will do.

I think too often we, as people, don't accept the WHO of God. We say it, but we don't fully grasp what John meant in 1 John 4, when he said that God is love. We improperly read 1 Corinthians 4, when Paul tells us what Love is, that it's patient and kind, that it doesn't envy and isn't proud. We misread it when we read that love does not dishonor and that it's not self-seeking, that it's not easily angered and keeps no record of wrongs. We misread it when it goes on to say that love always protects, always trusts, always hopes, and always preserves.

We need to read it this way, that God is patient and kind, that God doesn't envy and isn't proud, that God does not dishonor and is not self-seeking, that God is not easily angered and keeps no record of wrongs. We need to read that God always protects, that we can trust God, that God is where our hope lays, and that God always preserves. That's a reason for worship!"

More than anything, I talk about attributes of God between songs. I'll often take a word or phrase from a song and bring light to its meaning. I find this to be especially important because words seem to lose their meaning, or sometimes we forget their meaning. We forget their importance. We sing them, but we don't define them. For example, let's say I'm coming out of a song that uses the phrase "You are holy" multiple times, I might say this:

"The word Holy here speaks to the purity of God, the perfection of God. To be holy means to be separate, to be different, in a unique and special way. A way that is beyond us as human beings. In Hannah's prayer in 1 Samuel 2, she says "there is no one holy like the Lord, there is no one beside you." What Hannah is saying is that there is no one as perfect as our God. There is nothing that can stand against Him. There is no one who can compare to Him."

You could spend weeks teaching about the different attributes of God's character, which may not be a bad thing to do. Using scripture, define the attribute and speak to what it means to us as followers of Jesus. Don't be afraid to keep it simple, sometimes that may be what is best.

Names of God

In the same light, I often teach on different names of God. Again, I usually do this between songs, relating the topic of the song to a name of God. For example, if I am leading a song that talks about that satisfying nature of God, something that says "Your love satisfies," I may talk about a less common name of God, El Shaddai, which translates to God Almighty.

"In Genesis chapter 17 we read the first of 7 times that God is referred to as El Shaddai; which means God Almighty or All Sufficient One. In fact, it's how He refers to Himself. In the statement of His name, God lays out a promise to satisfy and sustain, to play the role of both mother and father.

Genesis 17:1

When Abram was ninety-nine years old, the LORD appeared to him and said, "I am God Almighty (El Shaddai); walk before me faithfully and be blameless."

Shaddai comes from two ancient words: Shad meaning breast; a source of nourishment and Sadu, meaning mountain; an image of strength. When God gives himself the name El Shaddai, it is just before He makes the first covenant with Abraham. As He gives instruction, He promises to fulfill His part. He promises that His people will be supplied for and sustained. He is promising life.

In Genesis 35, God refers to Himself again as El Shaddai. This time, He is blessing Jacob and calling him Israel. He is laying out the same promise He did to Abraham. This is a promise of future blessing, of sustenance; a promise of strength and of nourishment. God continues to promise life.

Genesis 35:11-12:

[11]And God said to him, "I am God Almighty (El Shaddai); be fruitful and increase in number. A nation and a community of nations will come from you, and kings will be among your descendants. [12] The land I gave to Abraham and Isaac I also give to you, and I will give this land to your descendants after you."

This promise does not stop with Abraham and Jacob. Matthew 1 begins by showing us the genealogy of Jesus. That He is a son of Abraham and an inheritor of the promise given to him. Because of Jesus, you and I are inheritors of the same promise. God Almighty is the God of strength and sustenance."

There is a name of God associated with nearly every promise of God. When worshiping God, both by name and according to His promises, He suddenly becomes much more personal. You begin to realize what He's done, what He's doing, and what He will do. Spend time teaching His names.

How to Worship

The third item I most frequently teach on, in regards to worship, is how we worship or the actions of worship. When discussing the Levites, I touched on the idea of modeling worship and discussed how King David instructed the Levites to praise God. We should constantly be modeling worship, but also giving instruction on how to do so. I often teach on why we do what we do, actions such as singing, the lifting of hands, and falling on our knees. The following are common ways I teach this:

Why We Sing

"In 1 Chronicles 16:8-11, King David instructs the Levites to give praise to God in this manner: by proclaiming His name, making known what He has done, by singing praise to Him, by giving glory to His holy name, by rejoicing, and by seeking his face always. This is why we sing! We're giving glory to our God as we seek His face."

Lifting Hands

"All over the bible, we find individuals lifting their hands in worship. It's almost a way of reaching out to heaven for a touch from your Creator. It's a posture of worship that says both "I love you" and "I need you." It expresses adoration and surrender.

Psalm 134 says "Lift up your hands in the sanctuary

and bless the Lord" Here, the psalmist demonstrates his adoration through his physical expression.

When Moses lifts his hands in Exodus 17, he is showing the dependency has on God. In this moment, the Amalekites are attacking the Israelites. Moses realizes that the Israelites have no chance without God on their side. So he lifts his hands, surrendering to God."

Kneeling

"In Luke 22: 41-42 we find Jesus on His knees in prayer on the Mount of Olives. This is just before His arrest. He drops to His knees in surrender to God and then proceeds to voice His surrender by saying "not my will, but yours be done." We kneel and give control to God. We kneel in an act of surrender, an act of humility before God. Kneeling acknowledges the authority of our All-powerful God. We kneel in demonstration of our recognition of the One True King."

Personally, I find great importance in the posture of worship. Through expressive worship, we follow a biblical example of worship. Through expressive worship, we worship with all of our being, as commanded in Deuteronomy 6:5.

As a worship pastor, don't miss the opportunity to teach on the subject of worship. Teaching will grow your congregation spiritually. Teaching will build a worshiping church. I believe it is necessary in order to pastor, to shepherd, well.

What to Remember

Leaders of worship, pastors of worship, ought to be teachers of worship.

Keep your teaching simple.

The names and attributes of God speak to why we worship Him.

When worshiping God, both by name and according to His promises, He suddenly becomes much more personal.

Direct your congregation in how to worship.

Teaching on worship will build a worshiping church.

Lead Yourself Well
Chapter Nine

A pastor's job is to shepherd people, to guide them and lead them, to serve them. We find the qualifications for this role in 1 Timothy 3 and Titus 1. Many of us have read through these in our study time and in every job description for church leaders that we have ever seen. Qualifications such as being honorable, self-controlled, respectable, and hospitable.

What we too often overlook when reading these passages, at least I do, is in 1 Timothy 3:1, that whoever desires this desires a noble task. I think this is important to remember, that it is a noble task, an honorable task, and we have been placed in this role for a purpose.

I read through the qualification passages at least once a year. I have since before I was in full time ministry.

Usually, around New Year's when I am planning, praying, and preparing for the coming year, I read through these passages to have a clear mindset regarding what I need to be in order to be qualified for the task ahead. Starting with scripture gets my heart right for the other growth steps I take.

Personally, I am passionate about becoming a great pastor. I have strong desire to be the best leader I can be. I want to fulfill the purpose God has placed me in this position for. In order to become a great pastor, I know I need to grow. I know that great leaders are growing leaders. In order to grow, I need to consistently evaluate myself and my abilities. I need to lead myself well in order to lead others well.

I am constantly seeking out ways to grow. The first way I do this is by seeking out best practices of great leaders. I read books, listen to podcasts, and meet with as many leaders as I can, from household names to local ones. I want to know what these people are doing to grow and I want to emulate it.

The number one best practice I hear great leaders talk about is reading. Find a solid leader and listen to him talk for more than ten minutes, I guarantee he will bring up a book. Great leaders always seem to be reading. They always seem to be learning. What I find most interesting is how often I hear leaders talk about books that have nothing to do with their field. I've talked with pastors who read about brain surgery and business owners who read about ministry. These leaders are seeking knowledge and understanding in areas outside of their profession. Their personal growth spills over into professional growth. Find leaders like that, in and out of ministry, and find out what they are doing to grow.

When I find people like that, who are always learning and growing, I seek to build a relationship with them. I want to surround myself with people who are better than I am. I want to find mentors who can grow me. We talked about this earlier when discussing Barnabas and Paul, but I'm not sure I can stress the importance enough. Find someone who is growing to help grow you. In this case, you may want to find someone in your field, another pastor, or at least someone who knows the Church well. This should be a person who can speak into your struggles and your goals as a pastor.

I would also encourage you to find a mentor who does not work alongside you in your current position. Although I hope your lead pastor or a campus or associate pastor is pouring into you, I've found great value in someone pouring into me who is not associated with my current job. Having a mentor who is removed from your workplace allows more freedom in conversation. It will sometimes allow you to voice any struggles, fears, or concerns more frankly. It will take away any workplace politics or agenda. A mentor who is removed from the workplaces allows for an outside voice to speak into whatever may be going on, good or bad.

Outside of the best practices of other leaders and finding mentors, there are a three items I try to remain constant in growing in: prayer, bible, and music. That probably seems obvious, but there are specific prayers I am always praying and specific books of the bible I am always reading.

When it comes to prayer, I pray for focus and humility. One of my mentors, Joel, said this: "Empty hearts, prayer-less spirits, and selfish motives have ruined far more worship services than all the activity of hell." I believe that to be true, so I often pray for focus on Jesus and a humility on the stage. The last thing I want is for a worship service to become about me, which is a clear danger with worship pastors. Early on in my ministry a pastor friend, Chip, told me that he believes worship pastors are under more spiritual attack than anyone else. I once heard another well respected pastor say that worship reminds satan of who he was.

I am not one that believes the devil is hiding behind every bush. In fact, I think many Christians spend too much time being scared of hell and too little time resting in Jesus. However, I do believe it is important to pray a sort of spiritual protection over yourself as a pastor and over your team.

On another note, a personal prayer I often pray is this: "Lord, make me bold like Peter, constant like Paul, and wise like Solomon." I always want to be praying for more boldness to preach the gospel, I always want to be prayed up and connected with God, and I always want be living a life of wisdom. I believe praying for these things has benefited my ministry. I believe it will continue to. Praying this three-part prayer daily has given me three daily challenges. I hope it challenges you as well.

I stay focused, and hopefully humble, by staying in the Word. There are two books of the bible that as a worship pastor, I believe are necessary to be actively reading at all times: The Psalms and Proverbs.

The psalms are the language of worship. The psalms are responsible for nearly every worship song ever written. In worship song after worship song, from Hillsong to hymnals, you can find lyrics from the psalms. The psalms teach us how to worship, from physical expression to language that glorifies God. The psalms teach us how to worship in the good times and bad. The psalms can teach us to write better songs. The psalms should be a language, we as worship pastors, are fluent in.

The proverbs were designed to give us wisdom, they are essentially one liners of truth. In my ministry there have been a large number of circumstances that have led me to pray for wisdom, as we are instructed to do in James 1:5; However, many times when I have prayed for wisdom, God has pointed me to the resources he has already given me, the book of Proverbs. I've found that reading a proverb a day (or two or five), has made my life much easier. It has allowed me to lead wisely and to grow in knowledge of the Kingdom. King Solomon was the wisest man to have ever lived. God gave him an unsurpassed amount of wisdom and Solomon wrote it down. How foolish would I be to not read it? Great leaders lead with wisdom. The proverbs teach us to do just that.

The last item I stay constant in growing in is music. Music is the biggest tool I use as a pastor, so I want to steward my competency in it well. As with leadership, one of the top resources I try to tap into with music is other musicians, better musicians. Play with better musicians often. The growth you will experience will shock you.

Like many, my main instruments are acoustic guitar and vocals, so I actively seek out better guitar players and vocalists to play and sing with. This has allowed me to maintain a steady amount of growth in my primary areas of focus. It has taught me harmonies, new guitar parts, and all around better musicianship.

Along with growing in my primary instruments, I am always searching to learn more about the other instruments played on my stage. I am nowhere near where I would like to be as a bass player, keys player, or lead guitar player, but learning more about these instruments, how they are played, and the equipment they use, has allowed me to communicate more effectively with my team. Better communication has made my team better.

Through my learning process as a musician, seeking out better musicians, learning my own instrument better, and learning other instruments, I have learned to look at practice as a spiritual discipline. Like I said, music is my biggest tool. I use music to incite spiritual growth in my church. I need to learn to use that tool well.

Growth is essential to good leadership. If you stop learning, you will soon stop growing. As a worship pastor, there are four areas you should constantly be growing in: Worship, Leadership, Music, and The Word. Read books, go to conferences, connect with great leaders, always have a mentor, and spend more time with Jesus. By doing these things, you will learn the best practices of worship leading. You'll benefit, your church will benefit, and ultimately, the kingdom of Heaven will grow.

What to Remember

Whoever desires this role, your role, desires a noble task.

You have to lead yourself well in order to lead others well.

Great leaders always seem to be reading.

Have a mentor who is outside of your current job.

Pray for focus and humility.

Actively read Psalms and Proverbs.

Learn to use your tools well.

Constantly be growing in these areas: Worship, Leadership, Music, The Word

One Final Thought

This book is not a comprehensive study on everything it takes to pastor people. There could be, and in some cases have been, entire books written on any one subject that we've covered here. My goal has never been to tell you everything, but to give you a starting point, to give you a new way of thinking about your role as a worship leader.

For thousands of years the only people who led worship were priests. They were people who were well educated, well trained, and the best of the best in their field. Although, we don't have to be the best, I believe we should strive to be. We should strive to be educated and well trained. We should strive to lead better. We should strive to pastor well.

My hope is that by reading these few pages on the subject, you've begun to shift your thinking in regards to your role as a worship leader. I truly believe that when worship leaders become worship pastors, churches begin to change. When we begin pastoring in worship, congregations begin to understand worship. When congregations understand worship, they step into deeper communion with their Heavenly Father. When that happens, lives change.

I believe the world can be changed through churches who put their focus on worshiping the God of the bible. I believe this change starts with those on the front lines. Those leading. Worship leaders. Worship Pastors. It starts with us taking the time to learn about our role and pouring into our churches.

Let's become better great leaders of people, instead of great leaders of songs.

ABOUT THE AUTHOR

Caleb Holgerson is a Worship Pastor based out of Graham, North Carolina. He has a passion for growing leaders and building worshiping churches. Connect with him online at calebholgerson.com or on social media @calebholgerson.

End Notes

1. Unless otherwise noted all Scripture quotations are from THE HOLY BIBLE, NEW INTERNATIONAL VERSION®, NIV® Copyright © 1973, 1978, 1984, 2011 by Biblica, Inc.® Used by permission. All rights reserved worldwide.

2. Other scripture quotations are from: Scripture taken from *The Message*. Copyright © 1993, 1994, 1995, 1996, 2000, 2001, 2002. Used by permission of NavPress Publishing Group.

3. Stanley, Andy. *Next Generation Leader*. New York: Multnomah Books, 2003. Print.

Made in the USA
Monee, IL
31 July 2020